What

Kristi Neace has accom
wives to share their feeli~~.~~ ~~...~~ ~~.....~~
stressful professions in the world. Worries about job risks,
financial hardships, shift changes and marital strains are hard on
any marriage; law enforcement exacerbates the problem. We call
their spouses heroes; perhaps we should include these wives and
their children in that group.

Grant Wolf
Executive Director
Fellowship of Christian Peace Officers-USA
Sr. Chaplain, Chattanooga TN Police Department

*"A superb project!"Lives Behind The Badge" has opened the hidden
area of spousal stresses and personal stories that give peace officer
support personnel the encouragement to voice their feelings. This
compilation of responses greatly assist our ongoing effort of
Christian ministry to LEO families and can become a timeless tool to
expose attitudes and concerns that might aid in the healing of hidden
previously unspoken "Post Traumatic Stress Disorders. I believe that
this book actually encourages dialogue from support personnel who
potentially suffer untreated stress as does the LEO in this world of
demanding and unforgiving law enforcement." Thanks, Kristi, for all
you have done to help this noble profession.*

Tim Eldred, Law Enforcement Chaplain
Rutherford County SO, TN
Christian Law Enforcement Summit
Coordinator/Director
LifeWay Ridgecrest Conference Center
Ridgecrest, North Carolina

God Bless!
Kristi
Jeremiah
29:11-13

When I was a small boy I had many heroes, Superman, The Lone Ranger, and Zorro to name a few. I didn't realize until much later that all of my heroes had something in common. They were the 'Good' guys. They righted wrongs, stood between good and evil and defended the weak. There weren't very many of them, they were proud yet humble, always standing out in a crowd, serving the public.

Perhaps, being influenced by my 'heroes' is the reason I spent 36 ½ years as a police officer.

As you read the following pages of this book try to remember that tonight, as you and your family sleep securely in your home, in another home just down the street, a family member is absent. In that home only one parent is there to tuck in their children, the 'other' parent has chosen to wear a bullet proof vest under their shirt, to carry a gun, and to work all night in every kind of weather. While it is human nature to avoid danger, your neighbor, the police officer, actively seeks out the most dangerous people in your community.

The following stories are written by the spouses of these men and women who protect us. The ones who, during those long and lonely nights at home, taking care of their sick children, wishing their spouses were lying next to them in their warm bed, praying their loved ones will come home safely. These are the 'forgotten' ones.

Tonight when you lie down, if your loved ones are secure, if you are not afraid of someone breaking into your home, say a prayer of protection for the police officers that will be up all night in your community, and while you're at it, say a special prayer for all of those families that are going to bed while one of their members are missing.

To the families that serve: the scripture Matthew 5:9 reads, *'Blessed are the peacemakers: for they shall be called the children of God.'*
Thank you for your sacrifices and GOD bless.

Retired Police Chief, Donald Fowler - Missouri

This book has truly been a God-thing from the start, but I would like to especially thank Carmen Leal for giving me the idea.

I would also like to give a huge shout out to all the police wives who contributed stories or simply called or emailed, giving a much needed encouraging word. It couldn't have been accomplished without your assistance and input.

To Rick, I give a very special "thank you" for your extreme support and help with this project. You truly are my hero!

Lastly, thanks to my children for just being great kids. I love you.

Index

Introduction

I have never denied the power of God or the calling He places on people's lives, but I have sometimes waffled in my faith. On the wall above my kitchen table reads a scripture that says, *"With God all things are possible."* Matt. 19:26. I've lived that verse this year, and my faith has become rock solid.

In the fall of 2008, I knew God wanted me to write again. I had already published one book and several articles, but that nagging, gnawing feeling that a writer gets when she's without something to write began to creep up on me.

It seemed as if I was hitting nothing but dead ends as I looked for ways to get up and going again. It was somewhat like trying to get back in the dating scene after years of being shelved, and getting nothing but rejections. The Lord, however, had a plan.

Searching through the internet for a writers' conference, I just "happened" upon one that would be taking place two weeks from that moment in Shawnee Mission, Kansas. I couldn't believe it! I had always wanted to attend one, and this would be a golden opportunity, however, two weeks was little time to come up with the money to go, schedule the time off, and find a place to stay.

The more I struggled against it, the louder the voice inside my head sounded, "You *must* go." Casually I glanced at the agenda and noticed my friend's name listed on the board sponsoring the event. Zeta and I served together on a women's ministry team for our state, so immediately I contacted her to find out more about the conference, and if it would be worth my time and effort.

"Oh, yes, you should go" was her response. "You can stay at my house." Well, that was all hunky-dory, but how would I ever afford the huge conference fee? That evening as I was getting ready to leave work, I lifted my head up to the ceiling as if looking God face to face, and said, "Well then, if you want me to go to this conference, you will have to provide the money."

Not thinking too much of the conversation, I packed up my things and headed home. My daughter, Meghan, phoned me on the way and asked me to stop by and pick her up from grandma's. As I pulled into the driveway, she ran out waiving an envelope for me. Inquisitive, I fumbled to open it wondering if perhaps…no, no, it couldn't be.

Inside, a check was made out for the majority of what I needed to attend the conference. I kind of snickered to myself and said, "Okay, Lord. If you want me to go, then do it one more time."

I had to be at a meeting at church that night, so I gulped down my supper and sped back to town. Excited to share the happenings of the day with a friend of mine, I rushed down the stairs and entered the room where she was waiting for her class to begin. As I began telling her the story of how "God just might be at work," she opened her purse and pulled out the rest of the money that I needed. "Here, He told me to give this to someone who needed it, and that someone is you," she said.

I sat there in disbelief. He had actually made the way possible for me to go. Two different people had given me the exact amount I would need to attend the conference. There was no question now; I was on my way to Kansas City.

The conference was wonderful and I learned so much, but I knew there had to be a deeper purpose for my attendance. Carmen Leal, who was also staying with my friend Zeta, began talking with me one evening on our drive back to the house. I mentioned that my husband was a police officer, when she suddenly stopped me by saying, "You need to write a devotional for police wives."

Huh! I had never considered that before. It wasn't long after, that I started this journey by putting out feelers. The response was overwhelming and I was completely convinced that this was where God needed me to be at the moment.

After many months of trial and error, blood, sweat, and tears…well, no blood as of yet, but truck-loads of the other, it was finally birthed! Oh, glory hallelujah!!

The last leg of this journey has been even more exciting. God has opened the way for my husband and me to be a part of a Law Enforcement Summit that LifeWay sponsors twice a year at the Ridgecrest Baptist Conference Center in North

Carolina. Of all things, I am now ministering to police wives. Hmmmm. Seems like a theme going on here.

I tell you this long, sordid tale to remind you that first and foremost, God has a plan. He is not some uninterested, uncaring cloud-lord hovering above us in complete angelic bliss. No, He is real and active and has placed each of us here for the specific purpose to have a genuine, unmatchable relationship with Him. Through the call He places on each one of us, and for those who give their lives totally to *Him*, the rewards are endless.

My prayer for you is that as you find your way through this book, you will come to realize how much He cares and loves you, how much you mean to Him, and how awesome it is when we seek His face.

All things *are* truly possible.

Kristi Neace

Psalm 29:2

A POLICE OFFICER'S WIFE

....Author Unknown

A special kind of woman;
A cut above the rest,
That's A POLICE OFFICER'S WIFE,
rating her the best.

How many goodbyes are whispered,
joined with a fond embrace?
As duty steals her man,
for the danger he must face.

How often have meals been ruined,
or tender moments disturbed,
by a call for a special duty,
sparking loyalty unswerved?

It's a devil of a job,
for an angel like this,
Who, for the love of her man,

must forsake that kiss.

She can run a garden tractor,

even paint a room in need,

How she can stretch a dollar-

is a miracle indeed.

She's a mother, lover,

chauffeur, and nurse,

A living symbol of:

"for better or for worse."

Rich is the man,

reaping his rewards in life,

who chose to be the other half of

A POLICE OFFICER'S WIFE.

CHAPTER
One

Chapter 1

"The first duty of love is to listen." – Paul Tillich

I must have a defect! It seems that every time my husband begins telling me something of importance, one quick blink and it's gone into oblivion. It's as if I am seeing his mouth move, yet my mind is focused on the trash *still* waiting to be carried out, the lack of attention I have received that day, the kids yelling in the other room, or maybe something as simple as that fabulous pair of shoes on the cover of the J.C. Penney sale bill. Other times, I might just find that I'm not willing to listen at all, but rather allow my frustrations to get the best of me through a quick snide remark or sarcastic quip.

"You never listen to me," he protests with a quiver in his voice. Then it hits me, could it be that I have once again disrespected the man I love by putting *my* wants and desires before those of my husband? Proverbs 19:13b, 14b says, *"...a quarrelsome wife is like a constant dripping, but a prudent wife is from the Lord."*

I've been called a lot of things, but I never want to be related to a drip that won't stop. The picture here is of a wife, who is a constant source of irritation. Yet, what the Lord seeks is a prudent or wise woman who understands her husband's needs, and shows him respect through listening and wise replies.

God has always been big into respect; He ordained it in the institution of marriage. Ephesians 5:33, says *"...each one of you also must love his wife as he loves himself, and the wife must respect her husband."* Yet all too often, after the honeymoon is over, our words become careless and our listening skills grow to be sluggish and half-hearted.

A general lack of respect towards our mate is one of the first red flags of a more serious spiritual problem...the sin of pride. It's as if we say "My way is much more important than yours." That attitude not only demeans the God-ordained position of "head of the home", but shows a general care-less heart towards God, Himself, and His perfect plan for our marriages.

Marriage should be a sacred partnership where the husband does not "lord over" the wife, but loves her as Christ loved the church, giving himself up for her. The wife, in turn, should respect his position and honor him with her words and actions bringing the two together in complete harmony…love *and* respect.

Let's hold unswervingly to God's teachings of respecting our husbands, listening to him and placing his needs above our own. If we do, God will honor our obedience to Him and our husbands will be blessed by the change in us.

And what about the trash…well, it might just get emptied!

Respect

No Ruby

"Who can find a virtuous woman? For her price is far above rubies." Proverbs 31:10 KJV

I was certainly no ruby...especially at 2:00 in the morning. The light had suddenly popped on blaring in my still unfocused eyes as he excitedly rushed to my bedside. "You awake...I just helped deliver a baby!"

My husband, a police officer at the time with the Jackson Police Department, had been on nightshift when a very pregnant, very much in labor woman and her husband pulled into the department's parking lot. Rick and a few other emergency personnel arrived at her car just in time to fumble through the precious moments of childbirth as a little, wriggling baby girl made her arrival.

With shear excitement and rush of adrenaline, my man still grinning from ear to ear, danced before me excited to share the "good news". At any other time, I would have been full of questions wanting every last detail, however at two in the morning I was not so enthused; not even the least bit interested. All I could think of at that moment was myself. How sleep deprived I was from being a young mother of two toddlers who had to get up and start the day again in just a few hours.

Then I noticed it. The smile began to fade off his face as he saw that I did not share in his excitement. I realized that I had not been the wife I had promised to be. Here was a moment in my husband's life that was important to him, and I had put my needs before his. "Lord," I would later pray, "Help me to be the wife that you have called me to be. Help me to put his needs before my own and show him how much he means to me as I listen and rejoice with him during moments such as these." I determined right then and there that I would be ready the next time, awakening with the best smile I could muster and say, "Hey, that's awesome!"

Kristi Neace, wife of Officer Richard Neace, Union P.D., Missouri

I Can't Believe My Husband Feels Dishonored

"Then when the king's edict is proclaimed throughout all his vast realm, all the women will respect their husbands, from the least to the greatest." Esther 1:20 (NIV)

My son Andrew was having a rough afternoon; he was tired, he'd been disappointed by a friend and he had homework. He tried to hide the tears dripping down his cheeks as he gritted his teeth and completed his worksheet.

My husband JJ was sitting across the room watching football, occasionally glancing over at our son and me. I thought about something fun JJ could do with Andrew to cheer him up. Then I thought about how it would encourage Andrew if his dad recognized he was upset and "engaged" with him.

That wasn't happening. So, I invited JJ into the situation by suggesting he turn off the TV and come talk with Andrew. At this point, I was not thinking very honoring thoughts towards my husband. It got messy. JJ felt insulted. I felt frustrated. Finally JJ said, "Tell me what you want me to do."

So I did. Andrew loved my idea to go do something fun with his dad. In minutes, his homework was done. His tears were gone, and so was my husband. JJ was very frustrated. It wasn't because he had to miss football. It wasn't even what I said. It was *how* I said it. He felt dishonored by the timing and tone of my words. I couldn't believe he felt dishonored. I felt so misunderstood!

I calmed down and thought more about what had happened. I remembered that JJ's preference is for me to call him into another room away from our kids when I don't agree with him. He's also asked me to share my thoughts in a non-critical tone. It was very hard to admit, but I knew God wanted me to honor my husband's perspective and preferences.

Just a few months ago God had taught me the importance of honoring my husband through the story of Esther. Esther was chosen by the king to be his new wife because his first wife, Vashti, *dishonored* him. The king's advisers insisted the king remove the queen from her throne because they were afraid her decision to dishonor the king would influence other wives to dishonor their husbands.

That passage reminded me that, although I may not influence a whole kingdom, my daily decisions are far-reaching. As wives, our words, actions and attitudes towards our husbands influence many. We influence the kind of women our sons will marry. We influence how our daughters will speak to their husbands. We influence how our friends might talk to their husbands after hearing how we talk to ours.

So, now I had the opportunity to apply this truth to my marriage. I have to admit it wasn't easy. My pride insisted that I had the best of intentions. *I thought so highly of my husband that I wanted him to be the one to speak into Andrew's hurts and right whatever was wrong.*

Maybe Vashti had good intentions. Maybe she was trying to prove what seemed like a good point, but it led to her downfall. Whatever the case, a bigger point was proven: a wife's influence is far reaching when she dishonors her husband.

I couldn't change what I'd done that day. But I could change how it was impacting my little kingdom. With God's help I told JJ, "I'm sorry for dishonoring you," and I said it in front of my sons. My pride was hard to swallow, but it went down a little easier knowing that honoring my husband honors God, and also influences my sons who I hope will one day look for wives who will honor them, too.

Dear Lord, I want to be a woman who honors my husband, but it's hard when that means giving up my desire to be right. Help me to honor You, my husband and others in my thoughts, actions, words and decisions. I pray that my life would have a Godly influence on those around me. In Jesus' Name, Amen.

Renee Swope

* * * * * * * * * * * * * * * * * * *

My Warrior

I'm married to a warrior. He has been in law enforcement for over twenty years, and now works in a segment of law enforcement that is safer for him physically. I'm glad he is no longer in threatening situations each day, yet continues his God-given duty.

God has put a unique call on one like this. He longs to protect and make a difference in the world he lives in, willing to run towards the sound of gun fire and danger. He is eager to serve.

I'm married to a warrior. I feel safe, protected, and cherished by him. As a wife, understanding him is challenging at times. Why would anyone want to be in the middle of chaos, and be sad when he can't?

I've known my warrior for over two years, fifteen months of those through marriage. I love him and God has helped me understand his heart and attitudes. Every day, I see him being molded and shaped into the man God wants him to be. You see, He is preparing *my* warrior to be *His*. This will be my husband's greatest assignment.

I'm married to a warrior whom I love and respect with all my being and I grow through the power of God in my understanding of his heart. Mine has been changed by that power. As I watch God prepare him for his battles, He prepares me to be a hero's wife.

Diana Williams, wife of Police Detective M.C. Williams, State of Colorado and Fairplay PD

* * * * * * * * * * * * * * * * * * *

You Might Be A Police Wife If...

You say at least a hundred times a day: "Shut Up, Your Dad Is Sleeping!!!!"

You have bullets and handcuffs sitting on your bathroom counter along with a fingerprint ink pad.

You've ever used the phrase "Can you please move your gun; I have no room for my stuff on the dresser!"

You can reassemble a Kevlar vest faster than you can make a sandwich.

You've ever washed someone else's blood out of your LEO's clothes and not asked questions.

Your laundry consists of 50 pairs of black socks and 30 black t-shirts.

His calls to you from work end with, "hang on a minute, babe".......silence...click.

You've ever run screaming down the street in your robe, because he's forgotten his gun.

You've had to remind him to check his bag for spare bullets before going through airport security.

You automatically choose to sit with your back to the door in a restaurant.

You've reminded him on more than one occasion that his personal car does *not* have lights and sirens.

You start standing like a cop when you're waiting around for something.

You start identifying perpetrators when you're in public.

If you've found bullets in the washer and dryer.

You're having an argument and it turns into an investigation of him asking the same question, but in different words to see if you say something different.

You have given up on planning dinner, breakfast, anything because more than likely he will be late.

Your children have a fleet of toy cruisers and sing "Bad Boys" while they play with them.

You are far too familiar with the stench of sweaty Kevlar.

Your husband speaks in code (then I went to an 83...).

You celebrate holidays on the "wrong" day or at strange times.

You're riding around with him off duty and he sees a car with one headlight. He reaches for his lights and begins to do a U-turn, then realizes he's in his personal car.

You have to make sure that every shirt you buy for your LEO is long enough to cover his off duty weapon.

You suddenly find yourself in a headlock in the middle of your sleep, because your LEO is having a dream that he's taking down a suspect.

Your best friends are women from all across the nation whom you've never met in person, but only over the internet on a website for wives of LEO's.

You have handcuffs hanging on your headboard and it's not for fun. ☺

Your kid rides his bike around the neighborhood with a pen and tablet writing down the plates of all the expired tags, so daddy can cite them.

You have a dog that you can never leave alone with the children, because a running child is a lot like a fleeing suspect. He wants to take them down.

You sleep alone, every other Mon., Tues., etc....

- Author Unknown

❋ ❋ ❋ ❋ ❋ ❋ ❋ ❋ ❋ ❋ ❋ ❋ ❋ ❋ ❋ ❋ ❋

CHAPTER
Two

Chapter 2

"When one door closes another door opens; but we so often look so long and so regretfully upon the closed door, that we do not see the ones which open for us." –
Alexander Graham Bell

I don't know about you, but things don't always look crystal clear to me. I'm one of those who want my life to read like a roadmap showcasing every highway, mile marker and potential hazard along the way. Yet real life is not as easy to navigate, and no relationship sails along quite as smooth as we would like for it to.

Several years ago, I talked with a woman whose husband, a Police Psychologist, worked with extremely heart-wrenching cases. Day after day she watched as the stresses of the job took its toll on her husband's psyche. For the life of her, she couldn't understand why a man with such a great education would want to "waste" his life trying to help the worst of the worst, and even more, not be at liberty to share with her the details of his day.

Then after many months meeting with a child who had witnessed his mother's murder, God penetrated the darkness in that young one's life, removing all the bitterness and feelings of abandonment. Because of the hours sacrificed by this wife's husband, the child accepted the Lord and began releasing all those pent up emotions, choosing to walk in forgiveness and freedom.

Often, we get caught up in the here and now, the stresses of the momentary and forget to look at the bigger picture that God sees. Had the sacrifices not been made, the child might have allowed anger to build a footing for a future life of revenge and hatred. Yet, the seeds of kindness and love that were sewn brought forth a bountiful harvest.

A good way to look at is, we don't always see the eternal difference behind our deeds, but God walks behind us watering the seeds.

"So we fix our eyes not on what is seen, but on what is unseen. For what is seen is temporary, but what is unseen is eternal." 2 Corinthians 4:18

Perspective

Never Say Never

Perspective is a concept that the Lord has been in the process of teaching me for many years.

Almost forty years ago, while on our first date, a young man informed me that while still in the military, he was taking law enforcement classes to prepare for a career. I looked him in the eye and stated in no uncertain terms, "I would NEVER marry a cop!" By the way, I also once said I would NEVER live in Illinois. *Never* say 'never'.

Before our engagement, he dropped the law enforcement idea until seven years into wedded bliss, when he announced that since we needed to supplement our income, he was going to take a part-time police job he'd heard about. This was simply NOT going to happen. By now two children were in our lives, and I was less open to fearing for my husband's life than ever. I argued long and eloquently, I thought, and then he calmly replied, "Well, I might encounter a robbery in progress while delivering pizzas and *I wouldn't have a gun.*"

So, after a few years of part-time police work, I wasn't surprised when he began testing for a full time job in law enforcement, leaving his retail management job the minute he qualified. I've learned that certain things are 'in the blood'. It's futile and probably not even right to fight it.

Today, my husband is the Chief of his department and our two sons serve different shifts under him. Our daughter, all five-foot-three inches, works as a Forensic Psychologist overseeing prison group sessions for sex offenders and murderers. Needless to say, with the whole family involved it can give one a sleepless night or two.

When non-police people find out about our family, they usually ask if I'm scared all the time. I admit that when fear has been an appropriate initial response, I have been afraid. Before I process things and center myself in the Lord and in His perfect Other-ness so beyond me, my heart and thoughts can race. But I do not live my life in fear of 'the phone call'. I *choose* not to let it control me.

The phone call could happen. It is inevitable for some. But, as I recently said to someone, "I would rather be a woman who raised a man who was on the right side of the law, *even if meant a tragic loss*, than one who had raised the killer." No one gets off the planet alive. Better to be an honorable person who gave back to society, who was dedicated to serving and protecting, and who was *"...God's minister, an avenger to execute wrath on him who practices evil"* (Romans 13: 4) than to be the lawless one who aimed a gun at a badge.

Perspective. It's helped me to reach for grace sufficient for the day.

Judy Mannino, wife of Vito Mannino, Richton Park Police Department, IL

* * * * * * * * * * * * * * * * * * *

Always on Duty

Do not be anxious about anything, but in everything, by prayer and petition, with thanksgiving, present your requests to God. Phil. 4:6

I believe that as wives of police officers, one of the most important things we must come to terms with is that being a police officer is not just a job, but it is who our spouses are.

Realizing that Ken, as with all other officers, is a cop 24/7/365 has not been easy. He lives in cop mode all the time; everything from sitting and facing the door in a restaurant, to stepping into the role of officer whenever necessary, is the norm. He can't shut the door on that part of his life.

Five years ago our family was driving to Alabama during our vacation, and we were just coming into the north side of St. Louis. There was a stalled car on the opposite side of the freeway along the median, with a patrol car parked behind it. The traffic on our side was crawling along at best during rush hour, when all of a sudden across the median, we witnessed a semi-truck slam into the cruiser from behind. The officer was clipped by his car, and the cruiser shoved into the stalled vehicle striking a young woman. The woman was flung through the air, over the median and over my sister-in-law's car directly behind our van.

Instantly, both my husband and his sister, an Iowa State Trooper, stopped and instructed our families to stay belted in. Each jumped out of their car grabbing flares and first aid kits, and assuming police mode. My sister-in-law headed straight for the officer, and after finding his condition okay, began directing traffic. As Ken reached the young woman, he found that both her legs had nearly been severed.

After emergency personnel arrived and secured the scene we continued on our way. Thankfully, doctors were able to reattach her legs. It was good to know that my husband and his sister took part in helping, never questioning the opportunity to assist, but adhering to that automatic response.

I again had to remind myself that a cop is a cop 100% of the time. To expect him to shut off that part of who he is, asks the impossible. As wives, it is our job to learn how to accept that fact and make it a functioning part of our daily routine. Being a cop is a big part of what makes my husband the man I fell in love with. I'd rather hear the ugly parts of his job, than have him shove it down inside and hide it away.

It's all about perspective. To see him for who he is and to be willing to listen to him, understanding and acknowledging that things aren't always easy. I can give him the space he needs, without feeling that it is me that is the problem, but the job he is dealing with.

Lois Dales, wife of Ken Dales, Sgt. of Detectives, Altoona PD, Iowa

❈ ❈ ❈ ❈ ❈ ❈ ❈ ❈ ❈ ❈ ❈ ❈ ❈ ❈ ❈ ❈ ❈ ❈

CHAPTER
Three

Chapter 3

"God of our life, there are days when the burdens we carry chafe our shoulders and weigh us down; when the road seems dreary and endless, the skies grey and threatening; when our lives have no music in them, and our hearts are lonely, and our souls have lost their courage. Flood the path with light, run our eyes to where the skies are full of promise; tune our hearts to brave music; give us the sense of comradeship with heroes and saints of every age; and so quicken our spirits that we may be able to encourage the souls of all who journey with us on the road of life, to Your honor and glory." - **Augustine**

Has fear ever overwhelmed you? I have a phobia of summer storms. It's not that I don't appreciate the cooling rains and the great awesomeness of the clouds that bring refreshment, but it is the destructive force of the wind and the hail that frightens me.

One late, summer evening several years ago, I was awakened to the rumbling of the thunder. My husband was working the midnight shift and there I lay listening to the sound of the wind bearing down on the trees beside our home. My mind raced as I imagined every terrible scenario that could happen, neglecting to hold tight to the reassuring hand of my Heavenly Father. Finally, in my fear I began to pray. "Lord, please protect this home and this family from the winds that are beating down upon us. Keep us safe and remind me that you are here."

A few minutes later, a tiny voice pierced the darkness with a sweet melody. A bird somewhere alone in the dark and in the threatening storm found its song as it clung to the peace that God had given it. This was exactly what I needed to hear at that moment. Before long, I had once again been lulled back to sleep with the knowledge that the Great Storm Keeper would see me and my children through the storm.

Several days later, whether I read them somewhere or God placed them on my mind, these words came to me, "Faith is the bird that sings while it is still dark."

That little bird had something I did not…faith. Oh, Lord, may it be that I will sing even when my life seems dark and circumstances are frightening, for you my Savior, are nearer than I can imagine. You hold my life in the palm of your hand and cause even mine enemies to fall at my feet. I praise you for your great, sustaining power and your gentle, Fatherly love.

* * * * * * * * * * * * * * * * * * *

Fear

Cry for Help

"So do not fear, for I am with you; do not be dismayed, for I am your God. I will strengthen you and help you; I will uphold you with my righteous right hand." Isaiah 41:10

"Help! I need back up!" I heard the poor sap's cries for assistance over the police scanner while I quietly folded the laundry. I was a couple of months pregnant with our third child, and this happened to be one of the few rare moments I wasn't heaving over the commode in the bathroom.

"Gee, I hope someone helps that guy," was all I could think of as I continued to busy myself, our two young sons running back and forth down the hallway. Little did I realize it was *my* husband that frantically called for backup.

Rick had been on patrol not more than a few hours when he happened to pull over the wrong guy for a DWI.

This gentleman, much taller and stockier, was not about to be taken into custody that night or any other. He had a rap sheet a mile long and had already made up his mind that if he was going down, Rick was going down with him.

As they struggled for what seemed like an eternity, the man used his over-exaggerated features to wrestle my husband to the ground, causing Rick injury to his wrist and forearm. Though it was the man that eventually found his

 way to the local county jail, it was my husband that took the brunt of the frightening episode.

I did not realize until the following morning that it was Rick's voice I had heard over the scanner that previous evening. I believe it was God

sheltering me from what could have been quite a traumatic experience; His loving hand muffling the familiar voice on that old police scanner.

Kristi Neace, wife of Richard Neace, Union Police Dept., MO

Our Father

Our father who art in heaven
be not silent unto me,
Hear the words of my prayer
as I lift up my heart to thee.
My Lord, my God, please protect this man.
Give him the strength to do all that he can.
Give him the understanding he'll need every day.
Bless him with patience in every way.
Give him the courage, the will to survive
all the unhappiness in so many lives.
Oh Dear Father up above,
give him all thy heavenly love.

-- AUTHOR UNKNOWN

http://www.mdfallenofficers.org/police.htm

Just Wanted to Say, "I love you"

Living with a law enforcement officer is a new adventure every day. It has given me a whole new perspective on life, and the upmost respect for all men and women in law enforcement, along with their families.

Anyone living with an officer knows they have no true schedule, and at any point in time whether in uniform or not, they may be called to duty. The life and death situations they encounter each day are reality, and bring to mind so many thoughts of courage, faith, and in the end comfort, knowing they do it for the better of someone else.

My husband, Travis, has been in law enforcement for 15 years and we have been together for eight of those years. He has worked in several different positions all within the same sheriff's department, as patrol officer, detective, narcotics, traffic unit, and SWAT. No matter what job he has been assigned to, he always devotes 100% of himself to a good day's work of chaos. For some reason, Travis always finds himself right in the middle of everything. As he would say, "I'm just in the right place at the right time," though I think there's more to be said for that line – "trouble doesn't find him, he finds trouble".

There are so many experiences to write about, but one of the most frightening happened several years ago on a quiet Sunday afternoon. We were not married yet and had only been dating about five months, when he got called out for a suspicious person with a possible meth lab. This was nothing unusual, and of course never at a convenient time. He said he shouldn't be long and we would continue on with our plans as soon as he returned. A few hours had passed and I hadn't heard from him, so I called to check in, but the call went to voice mail. When he finally returned my call, he told me he was on his way to the hospital along with the meth head.

At first, I didn't think much about it until he said, "I've been stuck with a dirty needle." He explained to me he was searching a vehicle like any other time, when he noticed a needle stuck down between the seats. Even though he was wearing protective gloves, it still penetrated through the glove and into his skin.

At the time, I was new to all of these situations and had no idea how this could affect him. Once I arrived at the hospital, he didn't have to say anything. I could see by the look of anger and worry in his eyes that something bad could come of it, yet was still trying to be professional.

He explained to me that the hospital staff were taking several different blood tests and would be putting him on precautionary medication for HIV and Hepatitis. The medication would of course make him sick, and so the waiting game began. It was going to be a long few days before finding out the test results.

Lots of emotions, what if's, prayers, and sleepless nights were with us those next few days. Everyone says there is always something good that comes out of a bad situation, and for me, it ended up to be one of the best of my life. It was at that point in time that I decided no matter what the outcome, I loved him and wanted to be with him for the rest of our lives.

The day came to go to the doctor's office to get the test results. It seemed like forever sitting in that office, we were finally given the good news that he should be just fine, though he would have to have regular blood tests done for the next five to seven years to make sure there were no long term effects. It was a moment that neither of us knew whether to smile or cry. So instead, we were both just silent for a moment. Prayer and faith are both so very powerful. Three months later, we were engaged to be married.

Even though being married to a law enforcement officer hasn't always been easy, I feel very privileged. No matter what may happen, I know I'm never alone. Our friends from the law enforcement community truly are our family, and are always there willing to support one another with whatever may come. We may not have much in common, but we all share one common interest. We love someone that is willing to risk their life to help or protect another that they don't even know.

I am proud to be one of these wives. The emotional roller coaster is hard a lot of days, but I know God is always watching out for him and I have a lot of faith.

There's just something about that interrupting phone call in the middle of the work day that you know can't be good. He's on the other end and simply says, "We're in a bad situation; just wanted to say I love you."

Maria Blankenship, wife of Cpl. Travis Blankenship,
Franklin Co. Sheriff's Dept., Union, MO

※ ※ ※ ※ ※ ※ ※ ※ ※ ※ ※ ※ ※ ※ ※ ※ ※ ※ ※

Hang Tough

I have been the wife of a Game Warden (yes, Game Wardens fall under the category of law enforcement) for 20 years. My husband has been in law enforcement for 30+ years; this being the second marriage for both making the odds of survival even less. These have been 20 of the happiest years of my life, but also the hardest and most frustrating.

I have had a lot to learn as the wife of a law enforcement officer. It hit me like a rock that LEO's tend to be some of the most cynical people alive. Most have lost their trust in people and don't make friends easily, or necessarily care if they have any outside of the law enforcement profession.

I am a people person, so this has been the hardest for me to accept. I love people. All of them. Okay, maybe not all, but most. Without having a personal relationship with Jesus Christ, I would have never made it this long, let alone for life as vowed on May 6, 1989.

God has been my strength and comfort when my spouse has turned his back in frustration and anger over my not understanding him. During those sad times, I've drawn extremely close to the Lord and have felt His power in my life stronger than ever. *He* has to be your closest confidant all the time not your spouse; even more so when things seem to be falling apart. I find comfort in knowing the Lord understands my deepest concerns and feelings, even when my husband doesn't.

Find other Christian friends you trust and can confide in. Ask them to pray specific requests when things are tough. Pray for your husband's safety always, for they are more afraid than they let on. Hang on to your God with one hand and hold your spouses' with the other. Never let go! You need God and they need you. Hang tough.

For the glory of God-
Deb Humeston, wife of Chuck Humeston, Conservation Officer, Iowa Department of Natural Resources, Iowa.

CHAPTER *Four*

Chapter 4

"The climax of God's happiness is the delight He takes in the echoes of His excellence in the praises of His people."

– John Piper

The day had been hectic but we were finally here. Our boys and I sat down in the stadium seats as we waited in anticipation not only for the game to begin, but for the whole reason we had come; their dad was about to be honored with many other officers as a part of Law Enforcement Day at the St. Louis Cardinal ball park.

As soon as the announcement was made, a sea of blue and black uniforms marched with heads held high onto the ball field. My eyes suddenly welled up with tears as I strained to see my husband file in behind many other brave men and women. What an honor. Though probably most of the people in the stands did not understand or feel the same sense of pride I felt that day, the genuine respect for the badge was clearly presented.

As I stopped to reflect on the gratitude and appreciation for each of those officers and their unselfish acts of service, my mind raced to another who gave of Himself completely so that I might have an eternal, safe dwelling with Him; that is Jesus Christ.

One day, the Bible says that every eye will see Him, every knee will bow, and every tongue confess that He is King of kings and Lord of lords. At that moment, the tears will flow and my heart will flutter as He takes His rightful place of honor.

Lord Jesus, help me to always give you the honor and glory you so deserve. For even the rocks will cry out if I am silent and fail to give you praise. Remind me that you alone are to be honored and glorified, for you alone are worthy.

"I saw heaven standing open and there before me was a white horse, whose rider is called Faithful and True...On his robe and on his thigh he has this name written: KING OF KINGS AND LORD OF LORDS." Revelation 19:11, 16

Pride

I am Blessed to Call Him "Husband"

I would like to tell you some things about my husband, Donald Fowler, who was known as "Chief" for the Union, Missouri Police Department for 33 and a half years of his 36 and a half years employed there. With a thankful heart, Don was able to say that as far as he knew when he retired, all of his officers were Christians. He taught them to play no favorites in town, to always be fair and honest, and he *never* allowed cursing to be heard inside the department.

His officers were not only officers to him, but many were like sons. Often, one of them would knock on his door for a word of advice. They would tell him of something sad in their life and he would offer wisdom and encouragement to them. But it never stopped there, for he would go straight home to kneel and pray on behalf of *his boys*.

Every year when the fair came to Union, Don would pay a visit to the fairgrounds a few days before it opened checking every booth to make sure that any item with offensive or vulgar language was removed. At their objections, he told them "This is called a *Youth* fair…take them down!" and they did. He would come home saying, "I don't know how much longer I can make that happen". My, how times have changed.

During the winter months Don would be out in the Police car patrolling when he would spot a young boy walking in the cold without gloves. Pulling over to talk to the youth, he would take off his own nice leather ones so that this child could be warm. Deeds like these never made the news, but made a difference in the lives of others.

Often a young man came through the town homeless, hungry, and needing money. The Chief would feed him, then drive him to the interstate, leaving him with some good advice and all the money he had in his wallet. He loved the opportunity to do this.

Don was also a hands-on Chief. When he was sitting in the comfort of his office and heard his officers get a call on the scanner, he would grab his hat and usually be the first one on the scene instead of staying in the safety of his office.

When the time came for him to retire, Don was ready. For over 2 years now, he has enjoyed his retirement, but each night his wife still hears him call out his officers' names as he says his nightly prayer. I am blessed to call him "Husband".

Dianna Fowler, wife of Retired Chief Donald Fowler of Union Police Dept., Union, MO

❊ ❊ ❊ ❊ ❊ ❊ ❊ ❊ ❊ ❊ ❊ ❊ ❊ ❊ ❊ ❊ ❊ ❊

Loving a Police Officer

Watching my love put on his uniform,
I catch the glint off the badge which adorns.
Checking his gun, adjusting his belt,
Anguish begins to build like the other nights I've felt.
I know his job is to protect and to serve,
And my mind knows good men are what the force deserves.
But selfishness enters with matters of the heart and so why him?
To put his life on the line for so many unappreciative women and men.
But that one difference is all he wants to make,
From easing some abuse to giving a lucky motorist a break.
So when his hand reaches for the door to begin his night,
Only God knows what will be his plight.
I can only hope he knows of all my love,
And in another breath say a prayer to God above.
Keep him safe as well as his other fellow brothers,
May they all return to their wives, husbands, and mothers.
But in the night I know a siren will wail,
For the call of duty will always prevail.
Injustice seems to need no rest or sleep,

But instead constantly lurks in the shadows deep.

Nothing matches the feeling at the end of his work day,

When he reaches out to touch me in the bed where I lay.

Peace reaches my soul and I thank God again

For bringing my love safely back to me, our family, and friends.

-- AUTHOR UNKNOWN

http://www.mdfallenofficers.org/police.htm

"On the Front Lines...Making Our Town a Better Place"

Where do I even start to tell you about this journey we began 20 years ago? I remember the excitement my husband and I felt when Kyle went to the police department and filled out an application. I say that lightly as the application was more like a book, not to mention a huge intrusion into our personal history. We both had high hopes and dreams of making a better life for our children than either of us had. Kyle especially had a very hard childhood with a drug addict and criminal for a mother for the better part of his life, and a non- existent father figure.

I remember the day that he took his application and gave it to Chief of Police, at the time, Don Fowler. Due to his family history, Kyle had neglected to fill out the entire application as he felt that it was a futile attempt at something better. Thankfully, Don called him and asked him why his application had not been filled out completely. Kyle spoke to the Chief about his childhood, and explained that he wanted to do something good but felt that it was a lost cause. My husband explained that given his family history, he felt there was no hope of him obtaining the position that was available. Knowing there were several reserve officers in the running deepened his concern.

Prior to his confirmation as the next patrol officer for Union Police, Kyle had been a newly saved Christian. He sat outside working on the riding mower and began to pray to God for guidance. He prayed that if it was God's will for him to become an officer, he would do it even though he was apprehensive. "If this is what you want for me, I will trust you to take care of me and my family and I will serve you all the days of my life," he prayed.

But even in the face of all of the family baggage, we sat feverishly in front of the television the night that the Chief was to announce his choice of the candidates.

I myself had a lot of mixed feelings in play... excitement at the thought of building a better life, and a fear of the man I love in harm's way. Regardless of my anxious thoughts, I sat beside him that night on pins and needles waiting to see what fate would have for us and our future.

At the time we had two small children, a daughter age 4, and a son 7 months, and we had just bought our first home. I remember looking at the children and thinking to myself "I can't raise these babies without the man I love," my mind battling between reason and a fear that seemed to creep in every time I sat still long enough.

We hardly spoke a word as we awaited the announcement...then finally we heard it, Kyle had been chosen! Sitting there in disbelief staring at each other, we didn't know what to do next. Reality quickly shook us back to our senses with the call confirming the news and giving instructions for Kyle's new job with the Police Department. A rush of excitement took over and we phoned everyone we knew to tell them, and the journey began.

Over the next few months we transitioned from photography to police officer. The local news papers reported "Local man trades in his camera for a badge and gun," and it said something about a different kind of shooting. Our lives would never be the same again.

When he first began working rotating shifts, it was

difficult with small children in the house and a husband who would wake if a feather hit the floor! What a challenge. We quickly learned that noisy toys were out, putting away any that made loud noises.

Even small amounts of light kept him awake, so sleeping during the day was not the easiest of tasks. We tried hanging blankets over all of the windows in the bedroom and blocking the light coming from under the door. We soon realized that it was still not dark enough or quiet enough for this light sleeper to snooze during the day. What to do...ahhhh ha, we had the answer.... aluminum foil on the bedroom windows, and a fan for noise!

We did our very best to hide the foil from visitors but I'm sure everyone still thought we were some kind of weirdoes! Oh well, it had to be done. He could not go out into harm's way with no sleep, not to mention the grouchy factor!

The last challenge to be resolved was the pitter patter of young children running and playing on the second floor of our home. Even with the carpet it was creating a thunderous commotion in our bedroom downstairs. Up went the baby gates. I felt like a hurdler just trying to move about through the house, getting my workout as I made my way to the bathroom.

Our living room became baby central, all toys, porta-cribs, changing tables, and swings into the living room in an effort to keep the rooms above the sleeping prince quiet.

As time passed, I'd like to think that we adapted to the changes very well. Life began to flow smoothly as we tried to meet the demands of Kyle's rotating 8 hour shifts. Then it happened. His training phase was over and he was assigned to work the evening and night shift.

For some reason, the fact that I would be sleeping alone did not cross my mind until this point. Did they not understand my intense fear of the dark and being alone? That was it. I would have to let them know that this would just not work for us.

I was panic stricken and searching for an answer to this seemingly huge problem. The days rolled on and the anxiety built as we approached the changing of the guard so to speak. Not only was I deathly afraid to sleep alone, but I was scared to death that my husband would be killed. For some reason the day shift did not terrify me like the night. I guess in my mind and with my fear of the night already, I felt that all of the bad guys came out after dark.

Unfortunately, I was not able to convince Kyle to not work the nightshift…like he really had a choice. The battle in my mind raged on as my first night alone approached. Kyle did his very best to reassure me, but I found no solace in the words he spoke.

I spent many sleepless nights laying in baby central (our living room) with my two children next to me listening to a police radio. I would strain to hear any word I might understand, as I had not yet memorized the 10-codes. I felt a sense of panic every time I heard anything sounding remotely dangerous, hoping that my officer would not respond to *that* call. But, he was always quick on the scene, and there I would sit clutching the radio close to my ear so it wouldn't wake the children. As soon as the call was over, a wave of relief would flow through me. It was absolutely exhausting.

As time progressed I over came my fears and eventually stopped listening to the radio all together. I realized that my husband had not just taken a job, he had answered a call. In light of the childhood that he survived, I believed he was the perfect man to make a difference. I also believe that God had called him to this line of work to use him to touch peoples' lives when they need it most.

I remember a case that probably affected him more than any case he had worked or spoken about. Kyle told me that following the investigation, he had difficulty for weeks, even to the point of withdrawing and becoming silent.

The case involved several young boys that had been molested by a relative of one of the children. The evening he got the call, he was out most of the night and I knew it had to be something serious, for he gave very little details upon returning home. The boys involved were the same ages as our youngest two boys; one of them a member of our son's sports team.

That Sunday, Kyle went forward at church to pray for the boys. I know prayer was a comfort to him, but he still had to work through the emotions that were created during the investigation. He finally let some of it go later on when we were at our local Wal-Mart and a young boy about 9 or 10 ran over to give him a hug. The boy told Kyle about something to do with school or sports, meaning nothing to me at the time. Yet later, Kyle mentioned how surprised he was that these kids seemed to make it through the tough circumstances. He would never forget the peace he felt when that child hugged him.

As a Police Officer's wife you share the same dramatic and inspiring experiences with your husband. There is no separation. When they are encouraged you are, when they are anguished you are as well. Sharing the experiences that my husband lives out is not a burden to me; quite the opposite.

I do recall though, that our relationship went through several phases. In the beginning I was anxious to hear every detail that went on during Kyle's shift; as time progressed I grew weary of hearing about things, but once he stopped sharing his experiences I realized how much I missed a huge portion of his life by not sharing in those experiences with him. From that realization forward, no matter how distraught a story, I was willing to listen and lose sleep with the Officer in my life.

Over the years our family has bonded in a way that only a law enforcement family can. I don't believe any of us would change things even if we had the power to do so. Our entire family takes a great deal of pride in the fact that Kyle is on the front lines fighting to make our home town a better place.

Stefanie Kitcher , Wife of Assistant Chief of Police Kyle Kitcher, Union, Missouri

CHAPTER *Five*

Chapter 5

*"The LORD is close to the brokenhearted and saves those
who are crushed in spirit."*

Psalm 34:18

"I pray I never have to experience that," I thought
as I sat glued to the television set. The news broadcasts
had continuously run the lead story about an officer fatally
shot. He had been sitting in his patrol car just outside a
familiar eatery, totally unaware of the danger lurking
behind him. It was sheer ambush.

My mind reeled at the thought of the widow going
about her usual activities at home, not realizing that at any
moment the knock would come at her door; her world
collapsing in one swift blow. Would I be able to withstand
the devastation?

Fear and grief overwhelmed me as I sat trembling
on the couch, my eyes misty with frustration at such an
injustice. Just then, I remembered that I am never
abandoned. That even during my darkest moments when I
face the stinging taste of death, I do not walk alone.

David, a simple shepherd boy who would later became king, experienced death of a loved one first hand on several different occasions. He penned a familiar Psalm that reminds us of God's unfailing love.

The LORD is my shepherd, I shall not be in want. He makes me lie down in green pastures, he leads me beside quiet waters, he restores my soul. He guides me in paths of righteousness for his name's sake. Even though I walk through the valley of the shadow of death, I will fear no evil, for you are with me; your rod and your staff, they comfort me. You prepare a table before me in the presence of my enemies. You anoint my head with oil; my cup overflows. Surely goodness and love will follow me all the days of my life, and I will dwell in the house of the LORD forever. Psalm 23

Dear friend may God always be your strength, your comfort in times of distress, and your rock when life knocks the ground out from under your feet. May He sing a new song over you and restore your joy.

Grief

"I Can Believe"

September 2005

My husband's death came as unexpected as a hurricane in Minnesota. And let's just say for a moment that if there could be a hurricane in a place without ocean waters, there is no evacuation plan, no rescue team trained for these scenarios, no logical solution. Because no matter how much you try, there is no strategy for unexpected, unexplainable disaster. There is no planning to prevent tragedy.

This is where I found myself, cast into tumultuous storms, raging to survive, and desperate for help. Out of place and territory, I felt the typhoon rip with crushing weight.

The day three officers appeared in uniform to deliver the report that my husband had been killed in the line of duty, my brain responded dazed, hearing the words but unable to translate, as if I spoke a different language. *I can't believe it* was the chant repeating itself in my mind.

He had put stop sticks on the highway to assist in a high-speed chase.

Accident? *I can't believe it.*
Deliberate? *I can't believe it.*

I loved him. Love isn't supposed to end this way. How does one repair the wreckage from a storm? How do I sum up love and my life with him, the life suddenly ended? Why didn't anyone work to save him, stop the storm, find him safety?
I can't believe it.

The suspect saw the police officer on the side of the road and swerved to target. My Shawn took three gaping strides. No human effort, no matter the strength or speed or stamina can outrun a vehicle driving over 120 miles an hour on a mission to take a life.
I can't believe it was my husband's life.

People quickly took shelter in my home, an instinct to find protection and help me care for our young children. Jordan was only 20 months old, and Madelynn was a five-month-old baby. We were all floundering. Throw out any rule books, we were all guessing. I took cover inside myself, numb and unresponsive. I wished for the rainstorm to take me too. *Let me die*, I begged God. Surrounded by more people than ever in my life, I had never felt so alone.

Within twenty-four hours of Shawn's death, I grabbed a spiral-bound notebook, and lying on my floor, I scrawled letters. My messages were full of significance and longing. *If I could talk to you today, I would not waste a single breath on things that do not matter.* For the first time in my life everything mattered and nothing mattered. Searching for meaning, I wrote. My body was furious, my heart lost. How can it be possible to lose your best friend and find any type of explanation to measure the loss? I didn't understand. Never before had life been so cruel.

As is true in any type of whirlwind, the scream for help is often unheard. Even with an army of people around me, I wasn't convinced anyone could hear me. The only voice I could hear burrowed deep inside me.
I loved him.

Where does love go after loss?

Four Years Later

My kids spend a week at YMCA day camp, cute little campers with sunscreen-plastered noses, dusty knees, dirty shirts and ketchup-rimmed smiles. Their counselors' names are Bubbles, Shasta and Twister. Jordan has a crush on the game leader, Kimgee. He tells me how she helped him with canoeing and archery. He shot a bull's eye on the first day. Maddi's love--swimming and singing campfire songs. They carry homemade crafts, kites and beaded necklaces.

As I drive home from camp, Maddi says to her brother in the back seat of the truck, "I wish daddy could pick us up." Her tone is nonchalant as if she's just asked Jordan for some water.

"Me too," Jordan replies knowing exactly what she means.

"Then he'd never be late cuz he'd have his police car..."

"And he could drive fast," Maddi finishes her brother's sentence.

I drive, peering in the rear view mirror wondering if I am really that late. I see thunderclouds forming behind me, drops of rain hit the windshield and I'm glad we made it to the car before getting wet. Self-conscious, I assume this is a reflection of me, until I notice how many other dads are coming straight from work to pick up their kids.

Maddi hands Jordan a bag of leftover pretzels from lunch. Taking one for herself, she tells him, "We wish our daddy could get us, right Jordan? But, he can't." "Nope, he can't," Jordan says.

It's then that I feel like I'm swimming in an Olympic-sized pool. The water blocks out the other noises of kids splashing, yelling, and laughing loudly. All I can hear is the vast, echoing swish of the water covering my ears. It reminds me of the rain stick we bought in Costa Rica; the one Shawn warned me was too big to carry home, the one he said he'd end up carrying on the plane.

But, I loved the hand-painted design and the soothing sound of small stones clinking against the web of sticks crafted inside to create a filter. I had to have it, and he rarely said "no" to me even when he was right (the rain stick journeyed back to Minnesota strapped to the outside of his backpack.) Mildly annoyed, he never said a thing. Secretly I think he liked the stick as much as me.

My thoughts sift and separate like falling pebbles. *One time I think.* Why couldn't he pick them up just one time?

"Mom," Jordan says as I drive around a cul-de-sac, "What does that sign say?"

"Dead-end," I tell him. "Oops...I took a wrong turn."

"Well, we need to find an alive-end then," he says.

His humor always brings me back and he doesn't even know he's funny.

"What's a rain stick good for," I ask, hoping this directs me.

"Making rain?" Maddi asks.

"Making a band!" Jordan says with limbs moving up and down as if he is marching.

Maddi has to think a little bit before she shares, "It's a magic wand."

The game works. And so we drive home in the rain accompanied by marching bands and magic wishes, rain sticks and life-filled conversations. This is how our life goes; the aftermath of the storm. Taking the *alive-end* route back home.

Where does love go after loss? Love remains. God uses love to sustain us, hold us close, move us and bring new strength. It is only by love that we can find new joys while honoring the love inside us. There is no tidal wave that can ever erase love. This is where my contentment lays—in the bright-eyed love of my children, the beautiful love of family and friends and the love of a life taken far too young.

No day is the same. In fact, life is very different from how I once knew it. I focus on the alive-end…the route that convinces me I still have a purposeful life to lead. *I can't believe it* once rushed through me like the waters of a broken dam. *I can believe* is my new message in the calm of the storm. I can believe there is still good to be found in life. I can believe I'm here for a reason. I can believe there in an alive-end route waiting to be traveled.
I can believe.

Jennifer Silvera – Widow to Officer Shawn B. Silvera (EOW 9-6-05) Lino Lakes Police Department, Minnesota

* * * * * * * * * * * * * * * * * * *

"*Thank you*"

"*…Weeping may remain for a night, but rejoicing comes in the morning."* Psalm 30:5b

I was married to a police officer twenty of our thirty years of marriage. I think the adjustment to being an officer's wife was a little easier for me than some, for we had time to get to know one another before Bill went in; our children past the stressful toddler stages at seven and eight years old.

Friends would ask me, "Don't you worry?" Sure, it's in the back of your mind, but I told myself that he was doing something he wanted to do; love for me was happy and proud. I chose to be supportive and not to fret.

About fifteen years on the force, Bill was made a Sergeant in his department; Sgt. Bill as he was known.

Around this time, a fellow officer and friend also named Bill, was shot and killed in the line of duty. It was like nothing any one of us from the department had ever experienced before; an extremely hard time for fellow officers and their wives.

Weeks later, my husband received a letter in his mailbox addressed to Sgt. Bill (Biggs). As he read it, it became clear that the author had mistakenly thought that it was he, my Bill, who had been killed. The letter told about the time my husband encouraged him to make something more of his life. Bill had a knack for talking with teenagers he came in contact with, often listening and giving old-fashioned advice. They could see his genuine concern and earned their respect in return. At first, Bill didn't recognize the young man's name, but later after searching old records, realized who he was.

Four years after receiving the note of praise, my Bill was fatally shot on a cold February evening. A wife can never truly prepare for that day when it happens. Yet, through the fog I knew it was just as hard for his sons, his mother and siblings, not to mention the department and family all over the country. Amazingly, I heard from people he worked with years earlier in Colorado, as well as kids he had been like a big brother to. Each one shared stories and good things about Bill and how well he had treated them.

As I began the arduous task of sifting through all his personal belongings, the letter from four years earlier came to surface. The young man's tribute to my husband made me feel good inside and I realized Bill had caught a glimpse of the impact he had made on one kid's life.

I am proud to have been a partner for so many years to this brave American and community Police Officer, yet the most special part in laying him to rest has been our family coming together stronger than ever forgetting not the legacy he left us.

Cindi Biggs, wife of Sgt. William Biggs (EOW: 02-07-08)
Kirkwood Police Department, Kirkwood, MO.

Goodness Under Pressure

*"Surely goodness and mercy will follow you all the days
of your life." Psalm 23:6*

I didn't know it then, but before my husband's accident, God already had a plan to care for me. I was far along into my pregnancy with my first child when my dad approached Porter and me with a heartfelt concern. With a new baby on the way, Dad advised us to invest in life insurance. It was a great idea, but we just couldn't afford it. Under the circumstances, Dad felt compelled to pay the premium until we could pay it ourselves. Porter accepted. Little did we know what the future held. Just two short weeks later, Porter tragically died. What would my son and I do now that our sole provision for food, shelter, and clothing was gone? The pressure was on as I tried to make sense of it all.

Sometimes God allows us to become pressured - not to terrify us or cause us undue pain but to purify our character. It's interesting that God uses pressure in our lives this way. In the same manner, pressure is what makes a diamond pretty, precious, and priceless. Diamonds are treasured stones that many desire. God wants you and me to become His treasured stones that shine with His glory. He uses the pressures in our lives to create in us a thing of rare beauty that many desire. When we allow the stress of life to purify our nature, we permit God to work for good and His glory.

Just when I thought I had to put my newborn son in daycare and find a job, it happened. It was nothing short of a miracle. It was God at His finest. Although the life insurance policy had only been signed two weeks before the accident and was still in the probation period, the company decided to honor it. Because of God's goodness, I was able to stay home with my son for a while longer. Sure, the pressure of my trial was hard, but learning to lean on God's goodness had its rewards. I saw a promise come to pass, my character and faith were sharpened, and I had the privilege of experiencing God at work in my life.

It may be different for you. God's goodness under pressure may show up in a job offer that you weren't expecting. It may be as simple as someone buying you dinner or offering to baby-sit so you can have some time to yourself. Whatever the form, it's His goodness showering you with care in your time of distress. Acknowledging these acts of kindness, which flow from God's heart, builds our character and our faith. Before we know it, our life shines with the brilliance of a diamond that draws others to our God. And that, my friend, is a good thing.

Dear Lord, sometimes my stress feels so heavy I think I can't go on. I have no breath or life left in me. But Your Word says that You make me lie down in green pastures. And Your goodness and love will follow after me. Oh, how Your Word refreshes my soul and renews my spirit. Be my strength; be my rest; be my ever-present help under pressure. With You, I can make it through. In Jesus' Name, Amen.

Micca Monda Campbell

Campbell, Micca; An Untroubled Heart, (David C Cook Publishing House, Colorado Springs, Co; 2009) Page 73

* * * * * * * * * * * * * * * * * * *

"Do not let your hearts be troubled. Trust in God; trust also in me." John 14:1

The Shield

A cop was killed one somber night, They buried him today.
He gave his life to do a job. A wooden box his pay.
Taps were played and the shots were fired That signified the loss.
They echoed 'cross the lonely land. All eyes stared at the cross.
The folded flag was passed along To his widow's shaking hands.
She held her daughter in her arms, And answered her demands.
So cry, my dear, don't hold it back, Don't lock it up inside.
We loved him so and he loved us, He served his land with pride.
He gave his life to do a job, That others could not do.
He proudly wore that silver shield, With pride we'll miss him too.

The young lass, with tear-filled eyes, Then turned and faced her mother.

This promise I give, I vow today, I'll never give another.

Some day I too will wear the blue And stand among the best.

I'll serve my land and do my job, Dad's badge pinned to my chest.

But if I too should fall some day, Fighting to hold that line,

Then take the badge from off my chest, Give me my box of pine.

And take that badge and keep it bright, For there will come another,

Who'll pin it on a shirt of blue, And swear that oath of honor.

And while he stands with lifted hand, His chest filled out with pride,

Beside and behind will stand the ones Who served, who fought, who died.

Though officers die, families cry, Others will come along,

To take the badge well worn with pride, To try and right the wrong.

It's those who watch while others serve, Who owe a debt not small.

These ones in blue, with silver shield, Stand firm, stand fast, stand tall.

-- AUTHOR UNKNOWN

http://www.mdfallenofficers.org/police.htm

CHAPTER
Six

Chapter 6

"There is no more lovely, friendly or charming relationship, communion or company, than a good marriage." – **Martin Luther**

"It's his fault! You don't even know what all he's done in our marriage." As I heard those words of hatred and hurt spill off my friend's tongue, my heart began to ache for this family. Not only had the ugly stains of selfishness and prideful spirits tarnished their marriage relationship, but now bitter feelings had built a wall around them. It seemed completely irreparable.

Little by little I had watched over the past several years as Lindsey had pulled farther away from her husband, John. She began absorbing herself in her career and working most evenings when he was home – not because she had to, but because she chose to.

Though her husband had been no angel over the last ten years of marriage, recently his heart began to seek the Lord, just the opposite of Lindsey. She, instead, grew ice-cold and withdrew herself from the encouragement and love of her church family. Little things began to bother her and everyone, she reasoned, was taking his side.

Finally, the last straw came when she opened herself up to "friendly" conversations with a recently divorced gentleman who lived just down the street from the family. As the visits lingered, Lindsey forgot the vows she had made ten years earlier to forsake all others and love, honor and cherish the man God had given to her.

John was furious. How could she have betrayed him like this? The hurt and anger drove him to his knees in frustration. He began to read in the book of Hosea where God had picked out a wife for Hosea the prophet.

Gomer was a worldly woman who lived an unfaithful life, and had even been taken and sold into slavery. Yet, God told Hosea to go and buy her back. Can you believe it? Too actually buy back his wife, and one, nonetheless, who had been so unfaithful? Hosea went and lovingly paid the price for his bride. He clothed her with his forgiveness and restored her to her rightful place in the home. God wanted Hosea to see the picture of how the Israelite nation had been prone to wander...to stray away from God and *His* best for their lives. Despite their rejection of God, time and again, He would lovingly bring the nation back and restore her.

John admitted that he too had been less than faithful - not through the attentions of another, but by setting Lindsey's needs aside in order to fulfill his own. Many hours were spent absorbed in sports channels or the internet, and he realized that he had neglected to be the spiritual leader of his home. Lindsey was often the one to take the kids to church and initiate the prayers before meal times. Why hadn't he seen the signs, before it was too late?

After several months of John's fervent praying, receiving wise, biblical counseling, and allowing God to change the habits of his old nature, his wife began to take notice. The two of them found ways to talk again and the lines of communication were ultimately restored. Submersing themselves in God's Word and building friendships with mature Christian couples helped them to heal their once broken relationship.

Lord, help me to remember that I have been forgiven of so many things. I do tend to wander away from you and try to find my happiness and contentment in things besides you. I blame my spouse when it is my own sinful drifting which has brought nothing but discontent and frustration. Help me to always put you first in my marriage, so as not to give the devil a foothold. Give my partner and myself the strength to stand firm on your truths and keep our marriage covenant pure. May we be a reflection of your grace and a light to many who are walking the same difficult journey.

Relationships

All Worth It

"Love means loving the unlovable--or it is no virtue at all." – G.K. Chesterton

I couldn't believe it was over. My husband and I had been married for 8 years when our daughter was born, and now six months later he had decided to leave us and move out of the house. Garry had been on the force for about 9 years at the time, when I felt as if my whole world fell apart in an instant.

My neighbor and friend who happened to be a born-again Christian (I had sold real-estate for awhile and found her the house down the block from us) kept asking me to go speak with her Pastor, but I was adamant that all was well and that I would be fine.

As time went on, and after Garry had been out of the house for over 6 months, I felt a new type of fear set in. I was frantic at the thought of giving up on him as most of my friends and relatives were telling me to do. I gathered my courage and went to the Priest since I had been raised Catholic, but sadly he could only give me ten minutes of polite listening, then asked me to wait 6 more months.

Life had never been so difficult and waiting was not an option. My friend's persuasion led me to attend her church where I met the Pastor who offered me more hope than I could ever imagine. He admitted that he had no answer as to why men do what they do, but that there was a book that could tell me the truth. The Pastor lovingly opened the Bible and shared with me the blessings of God's Word. We spoke for three hours, but the time seemingly passed without a blink.

I began to attend both Catholic and Baptist churches but after 3 months, I asked God to show me where He was calling me to be. It was simple, the Baptist Church was feeding me His Word and I was growing in my spiritual walk. I was saved and baptized on Father's Day, yet it took another 5 months before my husband returned.

We had a lot of people praying for us, and after he came home he spoke with my Pastor and was saved and baptized on Valentine's Day. Garry now serves as a deacon of our church, while I serve as a Sunday School teacher. We have had the privilege to counsel other couples who are experiencing problems due to the stresses of the job and everyday life.

Were the hard times worth it? Looking back now I would have to say yes. God used it all for His good, and our family is stronger because of it.

As a side note, we went on to have two boys; our eldest now attending Christian College to be a Pastor. Our daughter is married to the assistant Pastor of our church with a Grandson due January of 2010. God is good!

Judy Del Greco, wife of Garry Del Greco, Retired Capt. West New York Police, NJ

* * * * * * * * * * * * * * * * * * * *

I Believe...

I believe-
that we don't have to change friends
if we understand that friends change.

I believe-
that no matter how good a friend is,
they're going to hurt you every
once in a while and you must forgive them for that.

I believe-

that true friendship continues to grow,

even over the longest distance.

Same goes for true love.

I believe-

that you can do something in an instant

that will give you heartache for life.

I believe-

that it's taking me a long time

to become the person I want to be.

I believe-

that you should always leave loved ones

with loving words. It may be the last

time you see them.

I believe-

that you can keep going

long after you can't.

I believe-

that we are responsible for what we do,
no matter how we feel.

I believe-
that either you control your attitude
or it controls you.

I believe-
that regardless of how hot and
steamy a relationship is at first,
the passion fades and there had
better be something else to take
its place.

I believe-
that heroes are the people
who do what has to be done
when it needs to be done,
regardless of the consequences.

I believe-
that money is a lousy way of keeping score.

I believe-

that my best friend and I can do anything

or nothing and have the best time.

I believe-

that sometimes the people you expect

to kick you when you're down,

will be the ones to help you get back up.

I believe-

that sometimes when I'm angry

I have the right to be angry,

but that doesn't give me

the right to be cruel.

I believe-

that just because someone doesn't love

you the way you want them to doesn't

mean they don't love you with all they have.

I believe-

that maturity has more to do with

what types of experiences you've had

and what you've learned from them
and less to do with how many
birthdays you've celebrated.

I believe-
that it isn't always enough to be
forgiven by others. Sometimes you
have to learn to forgive yourself.

I believe-
that no matter how bad your heart is broken
the world doesn't stop for your grief.

I believe-
that our background and circumstances
may have influenced who we are,
but we are responsible for who we become.

I believe-
that just because two people argue,
it doesn't mean they don't love each other.
And just because they don't argue,
it doesn't mean they do.

I believe-

that you shouldn't be so eager to find out a

secret. It could change your life forever.

I believe-

that two people can look at the exact
same thing and see something totally.
different.

I believe-

that your life can be changed in a matter of
hours by people who don't even know you.

I believe-

that even when you think you have no more
to give, when a friend cries out to you
you will find the strength to help.

I believe-

that credentials on the wall
do not make you a decent human being.

I believe-

that the people you care about most in life

are taken from you too soon.

Author Unknown

❝ ❝ ❝ ❝ ❝ ❝ ❝ ❝ ❝ ❝ ❝ ❝ ❝ ❝ ❝ ❝ ❝ ❝

The ride

"Carry each other's burdens, and in this way you will
fulfill the law of Christ."

Galatians 6:2

Summing up 14 years of a marriage to a Law
Enforcement Officer, who has carried that title for 24 years
so devotedly and honorably, has not been an easy task.
Simply put, our lives have been a wild roller coaster ride.

Until the past year or so, I asked myself (and God)
nearly every day, sometimes several times a day, why this
"ride" was so crazy? Was it me...the kids? What about
quality family time, romance, happiness, and laughter?
What needed to be changed to achieve any of these, and
could it change? Were we changeable? Were we meant to
be? The questions, debates, struggles were never ending.
Help literally flooded in from caring friends and family
with words of advice, prayers, etc.

We turned to professionals as well, yet it was hard
for him to open up. Things were not getting any better and
we were still looking for the answer.

Thankfully, this past year the "ride" has calmed down and we are laughing, loving, and starting to again enjoy life at almost 50. It wasn't any one specific thing, just that my husband and I decided TOGETHER to get off the wild ride we had been on. We *both* wanted more out of life than the daily ick his job rebounded onto our lives. We made a commitment to one another to talk more about his job...my days...cuddle more...and literally date often! We rekindled our entire relationship all on our own—this time with no professional assistance--just the strong will and desire to stay together. We verbally listed those reasons and then...

...we agreed that we wanted to grow old together, experiencing and learning a lot more in life collectively.

May each and every one of you talk, laugh, grow and learn with your partner as you enjoy your ride to its fullest!

Eileen Wade - Always at (Don Wade) #720's side in Union, MO

* * * * * * * * * * * * * * * * * *

Making Time

Even after 32 years of marriage, I still remember the lonely nights without my husband at home, and the boys' endless asking when their dad's next day off was. Like so many others, I often filled the roll of both parents having to remember that he was working to provide for us.

Going to church without him was one of the harder issues, especially when well-meaning people questioned his absence. Yet, there were good things like getting our first cell phones. My husband would call me two to three times during his shift. It was great to be able to talk to him when I was having discipline problems with our sons. Sometimes he would phone just to say he loved us and was thinking about us, which always meant so much.

On occasion we would meet him for lunch. The boys enjoyed going to the station and seeing dad at work. Other times he would stop by in the patrol car while on duty to watch them play football or baseball. We savored every moment with each other and learned many hard lessons, the most important to never take one minute for granted, but cherish each day.

As a couple, we chose to make the effort to give one another a hug and say "I love you" before leaving for work. It's the small things that make up a successful marriage; the ability to adjust to change and the strength from God to be flexible enough to adapt to hard times. These are the two ingredients needed to have a lasting marriage and family.

Sharon J. Bickerstaff, wife of Deputy Nathan D. Bickerstaff, Ellis County Sheriff's Office, Waxahachie, Texas

CHAPTER
Seven

Chapter 7

"You kids are driving me crazy!" I often said that as a way to vent frustration. Not that I really meant I was actually going crazy, nor did they physically drive me that way, but sometimes when I was home alone with them...*again*, due to my husband's work shift, I just wanted to run away and hide somewhere for a very, VERY long time.

Why was it that as they were growing up *I* was the one that ushered them to ball practice and band concerts, fall dances or school plays? Why did *I* have to carve pumpkins and put together King Tut costumes? It was *I* that helped feed homeless kitties and bathed mangy dogs. *I* was the one that repaired a hole in the wall or put a door back on its hinge. *I* paced the floor during the dark of the night while my toddler screamed in pain.

Then it hit me...er, well, God reminded me, *I* was the one He had given all these blessings to. *I* was the one that He entrusted these three precious lives with, and *I* was the one that my husband chose with full confidence to care for such precious cargo.

In my pity party moment, I realized how much I had to be thankful for. God had blessed me with one terrific husband who was willing to work such long, tedious hours so that the five of us could enjoy all the good things in life. Yes, he missed many of the special moments because duty called, but it brought a smile to my face just knowing that he could do his job unafraid of what he might walk in to at his shift's end. I was serving not only my family, but my God.

Our kids are almost grown now - three of the most fantastic human beings at ages 14, 18, and almost 21. I actually observed them just the other day standing in the kitchen talking to one another in civilized tones...I never thought it possible!

Lord, *I* am the one that is so blessed. *I* am the one that you have showered me with such greatness. *I* am thankful.

"A wife of noble character who can find?...Her husband has full confidence in her and lacks nothing of value. She brings him good, not harm, all the days of her life....She watches over the affairs of her household and does not eat the bread of idleness. Her children arise and call her blessed; her husband also, and he praises her." Proverbs 31:10a, 11, 27-28

* * * * * * * * * * * * * * * * * * *

Thankfulness

"Life is not measured by the number of breaths we take, but by the moments...that take our breath away." –

Author Unknown

Enough

I was contemplating about what story or stories I should write. So of course, as with everything, I tried to think of what my objective was. What point was I going to make? I could tell you what it was like when TJ was shot. I could tell you how I have learned to cope with being the wife of an officer. I could probably give you advice on what not to do as the wife of an officer. I could tell you how I have managed children, a full time job, and a marriage of thirteen years. Oh the possibilities.

It has been two and half years since the shooting. It's funny but most of life's memories are tied to some milestone. For example, my third daughter, Rebecca, will always be thought of as the one born "after". After our hearts were broken, after everything changed, you know, "after". That would make my second daughter the *before*. She is my Grace. That's what I named her and that is what she is. You see, I didn't want to have any more children. Everything was great as it was, and I was TIRED. Little did I know how tired I could really be.

Grace came at a time in my life when I was already busting at the seams. What could I do? What could I say? "No thanks God, I have enough." No to God?! I think not.

You do what I did. You say "Your will be done, but for the record, I'm TIRED," smile, and politely nod. What I'm trying to say, is that I didn't deserve Grace. No one ever does. Yet God saw fit to give her to me. Here she is, my constant reminder that He knows just what I need when I need it. That's what I believe. That's what I know to be true.

There is a difference between head knowledge and heart knowledge though. Maybe God was testing me with grace; testing my faith, my willingness to respond to Him. My head has always known that being married to a cop could end up with me being a widow. I've always known this. I knew that it wouldn't be a matter of if I was called, but a matter of when. My head knew that the job was dangerous and fraught with peril (sounds like something out of a B rated movie doesn't it?) I knew because I had been living it for 10 plus years…except, I didn't really know. Not a clue.

It wasn't a phone call I received, but a knock. I had just gotten the kids to bed for their nap, and had just laid down on the couch for mine, then came the knocking. I'm not proud of the things that went through my mind while I was peeling myself off of the couch and going up the stairs to answer the door. Most of them were not very Christian, and most ran along the lines of "this had better be good".

My day had already been very frustrating and I'll admit I was pretty cranky and NEEDED that nap. I'm there at the door and whoever it was had not stopped pounding on it. It had been less than a minute, but the knocking seemed to have been going on for a long while. When I opened the door there stood S.P. The first thing that ran through my mind is that he was off duty because of his arm in a sling. He began by saying, "TJ is okay... He's been shot, but he's okay."

I stood there with a blank stare on my face. The few seconds it took for me to process his words seemed like an eternity. I wanted to ask him if he was seriously going to stand there and tell me that TJ had been shot. Had

I heard him correctly? Then he said "We have to go now. Come on. Carla is coming to watch the kids." My brain recovered enough to tell my oldest that I had to go, and grabbed my purse. Carla pulled in as we were walking to the car, and I tried to give her a few last minute instructions.

The drive over to the hospital was quiet…let me rephrase that, I was quiet. I prayed. I prayed any prayer I could remember; Hail Mary, Sacred Heart, and of course the Our Father. My mind was very calm, mostly because it was frozen; just like a computer screen when it tries to run too many processes at once.

I thought about TJ. In my mind he was just laying there, alone, waiting for me to get there. I prayed that God would reach out his hands and hold them over him, letting the warmth of His person, a little bit of His essence pour out and consume TJ's body and mind. Mainly I was concerned with how scared he was, and if I would be able to bring some small comfort that would get him through.

I prayed that God would reassure and comfort him for me until I could get there. In my mind, I tried to envision God's presence and comfort blanketing and covering him. That was my prayer; For TJ to know peace and love while he was hurting.

At the hospital I was taken to his trauma room and the look on his face when he saw me was one of great relief. My thoughts ran along the lines of "okay, he's conscious and aware which means we are good for the moment". I stayed with him for a few minutes to reassure myself that things were under control, and then began making the phone calls. My mom came first. I'm no different from most other children in that when I'm hurting and scared, I want my mommy. Next I had to speak with TJ's mom, and then his dad.

The next ten days that we spent in the hospital were difficult to say the least. I was in way over my head and scared to pieces. I managed to pull myself together with help from God, friends, family, coworkers, and complete strangers, but best of all, TJ and I made it home in record time.

We had quite a few visitors both in and out of the hospital. Everyone wanted to come and see my husband and offer support and love, which was exactly what he needed. He was so thankful to be alive, and couldn't wait to tell people how God had saved him. I believe that sharing with others really helped TJ keep a positive attitude about the situation, and heal quicker.

People ask me if I worry more now than I did before and I answer them "no, I don't worry more, it's just different now". Life after *is* different. There's a difference between head knowledge and heart knowledge and now my heart knew. It knew what it was to be broken and beaten. It also knew that God loved me and wanted what was best for me, and that sometimes that has to be enough.

Erin Wild, wife of Deputy T.J. Wild, Franklin Co. Sheriff's Dept., Union, MO

"I hear the footsteps on the pathway, the turn of your key in the door – I find my fears are unfounded – you are safe and home once more." – **Unknown**

Behind Them all the Way

Every morning that Derek comes home safely is a relief and a thankful prayer sent to God.

Two years ago, my husband's department lost one of their own to a car accident. It was the saddest, but most touching funerals I have ever attended. The entire department was at the funeral along with their wives or girlfriends; wives sitting in the back of the church behind their husbands. What a beautiful picture of support, not only for them but also for the deputy's grieving fiancé. I would like to think it is that way in our homes as well...behind them all the way.

Sincerely,

Jan Miller, wife of Officer Derek Miller, Charleston, WV

❝ ❝ ❝ ❝ ❝ ❝ ❝ ❝ ❝ ❝ ❝ ❝ ❝ ❝ ❝ ❝ ❝ ❝

Hand them Over

Many wives often comment about how their spouse changes after becoming an LEO. I haven't really noticed that in my husband, David, but then again he and I have been together since just before high school graduation. I think we sort of grew up recognizing the changes in each other, all for the best. Sure, he has had times of burn out when he is grouchier and more difficult to deal with, but doesn't that come with the territory?

We have often been told by others that we don't have a "normal" relationship. I was even voted the "coolest wife" because I didn't pitch a fit every time he was needed on duty, or when he just wanted to spend time with the guys. I realize that my husband needs that time just as much as I do with friends, so why should I complain. If ever I need him to stay home, all I have to do is ask. To me, that is a huge part of being a wife; to be flexible, understanding, supportive, and to keep the lines of communication open.

When David and I first married, we didn't attend church. God didn't play much of a part at all. I figured He would watch over my husband for me, and vowed not to let worry take over.

Shortly thereafter, my husband was in an accident in his squad car. He was headed to assist another officer and someone pulled out of a parking lot in front of him causing the accident. Thankfully, no one was seriously injured.

The most serious of incidents which tested my faith in God, happened when an officer from our department was killed; David would have been there, but happened to be on another call. One of our best friends lay on the ground, shots flying over his head. When my husband came home from work I could tell he wasn't okay. Something was wrong because he was actually crying. When he told me what happened, I wept for the slain officer and for David who was kept safe. Right then, it became real to me that the Lord was watching over him.

Being the spouse of an LEO can be hard and too much to endure at times, but the most important thing is letting God be part of your life and marriage. He can handle so many of the things that we can't such as worry and stress. We just have to hand them over to Him.

Kathy Everman, wife of Officer David Everman, IMPD, Indianapolis, IN

* * * * * * * * * * * * * * * * * *

Don't forget to Pray

I was asleep in my bed when for some reason I awoke. I began to pray for my husband, which I do on occasion when I can't get back to sleep. All of sudden, the house phone rang and I recognized my husband's cell phone number. I could hear as soon as I picked up the receiver that he was crying. He told me that he had just shot someone.

My mind was racing as I listened to him describe the details of that horrific night…it could have been him. I saw my life and that of our preschooler's flash before my eyes. What would I do without his strength?

My husband is all I've ever known and when I married him, I married my best friend. We both thanked God for sparing him, and then prayed for the family of the man whom he killed. My husband always promised me that he'd do whatever it took to come home, and now I believe him. This incident really changed our relationship.

We never take anything for granted, and are truly better off for the whole thing.

Behind every great man is a woman who helps make him that way, so to you, the wife of an officer, thanks for what you do.

Laura, wife of Scott, Bedford, VA

CHAPTER
Eight

Chapter 8

"Life is like a winding road. Some days it makes you nauseas, other days you want to find the quickest exit, but the one who determines himself to stay the course reaches their destination with a larger view of the world and miles of stories to share." – **Kristi Neace**

Glancing at her watch in disgust, Barb fiddled in her chair thinking to herself, "Here's another time that this job of his has taken him away from an important family moment."

It was their daughter's sixth grade band concert and Kelly had the flute solo in one of the songs they would be playing. "Why was it that every time something like this came up, Ron had to work?"

About that moment, Jill, came shuffling down the aisle drenched from the torrents of rain that had begun to fall outside. "It's a mess out there," she whispered to Barb. "I saw Ron directing traffic around that bad accident at the stoplight," she added. "It looked like someone was being taken away in an ambulance."

Barb suddenly felt a twinge of remorse as she remembered hearing the sirens blaring through the busy intersection near the school. She shamed her thoughts of selfishness as she pictured Ron, soaked to the bone in the pouring rain, helping those who could not help themselves.

As the students filed across the stage, Kelly excitedly waived to her mother finding her way to her seat. The concert went off without a hitch and the flute solo was a success.

As she and the other parents exited the school theater, Barb reminded herself that even though Ron had to make sacrifices at times, she was thankful in knowing that someone was benefiting that rainy evening from a kind heart and a calming voice. Was he really missing anything? No, most assuredly Kelly would give him a personal concert at home, but he *was* making a difference in someone's life that needed his help at that moment in time.

Thank you God for the sacrifices that these brave men and women make on a daily basis. I often take for granted all the hours spent helping those who cannot help themselves. Please teach me to be patient and accept the times when my agenda is interrupted. Let me be a sweet song of encouragement when the day is done, realizing that they are only living out your call.

Sacrifice

Following God's Path, Finding our Way

I was seventeen and had never had a family member in the criminal justice field. I met my boyfriend while taking college classes during my senior year of high school. Chris was in his first year of college and had plans to attend the academy. Neither of us knew what to expect.

Unlike some academies, my boyfriend was not required to stay on site, which became a blessing in itself. He was often teased because of our commitment to stay pure before marriage, and it was hard to stand for our convictions. I felt frustration in not knowing what to do or say to help him through.

When the academy was finished, Chris went to take the OPOTA test. He didn't pass. The next time he took it, his mom and I went with him and had the opportunity to pray together. If this was God's will, then He would work it out. After a four-hour-long drive back to his house, Chris received the news that he had passed. I was now a police officer's girlfriend.

I've heard a lot of police officer's wives and girlfriends say that when their phone rings, they freak, however I'm just the opposite. If Chris doesn't call, then I freak because we talk to each other every day when he's not sleeping.

One night I got a call at two in the morning. I was half awake and all I could hear was him crying on the other end. He told me that he had almost taken the life of a woman my age because of a stupid mistake he made. I didn't know what to say or how to help because I was so new to this police thing. I simply trusted in the Lord and believed that God would take care of him, giving me the peace that I needed at that moment.

However, the most frightening time happened when he wanted to carry an off duty gun, quite typical for guys on the force. Chris was taking it apart forgetting to pull the magazine out. Without realizing, he pulled the trigger like normal and the weapon fired. The bullet hit his hand and continued to penetrate through his dad's arm. God was in the house that night because no one was seriously injured, and both made a full recovery.

As with all relationships, there have been tough times and good times. Chris has had many thoughts about changing careers, sometimes not knowing what to do. As for right now though, he is where he is called to be.

Law Enforcement life can be challenging, but finding peace in frightening situations is a must and can only come from the Lord. He will give both you and your LEO strength for the tasks ahead if you will ask Him.

My hope is that my story has given you some encouragement knowing that there are others who understand what you are going through and the sacrifices which are made.

Britt Sharp, wife of Officer Chris Sharp, Williamsburg Police

* * * * * * * * * * * * * * * * * * *

"Linner"

Romans 12:2 New Living Translation

"Don't copy the behavior and customs of this world, but let God transform you into a new person by changing the way you think. Then you will learn to know God's will for you, which is good and pleasing and perfect."

I'd be lying to you if I said being married to a police officer was easy. Marriage itself is challenging. Married with five kids is like running a daily marathon. Being married with five kids to a police officer is like the extreme sports of family life. I'd also be lying if I told you I'd never dreamed of my husband having a "normal" job; a job where he could be home for dinner at the same time every night and deal with inanimate objects like cars or pipes, rather than soon-to-be inmates.

I have quickly found out that our "normal" isn't the "regular" world's way of doing things. We've pulled our kids out of school during the day to spend some midweek-weekend time as a family. We've celebrated birthdays at nine a.m. complete with birthday cake and candles after Dad worked the nightshift. We've waited patiently for him to come home while on shift to open Christmas presents. I've cooked a full dinner and dessert just to spill half of it on the floor of my car while driving all the way across town during rush hour with hungry kids, just to have a home cooked dinner with Dad. It's a lot like thinking of your family life as clay and molding it around a form, pushing it into the little spots and making it fit. It doesn't always cover; there are holes no matter what, and the job seeps through. The job of law enforcement pretty much calls the shots.

I'm totally convinced people at church think I'm a single mom. They see me tote all the kids in and out every Sunday by myself, using the special needs closer parking, because I'm literally in a full sweat by the time I get them all to five separate rooms in two different buildings, and myself to a third. When I finally get to that spot in the pew and can catch my breath, the solitude is so welcomed and appreciated. But after settling in and looking around at all the couples around me, I start noticing all the husbands with their arm wrapped around their wife. I start thinking that these couples may have had a date night and dinner out the night before and can go home and lounge around together on a Sunday afternoon. Jealousy starts rumbling a bit and, if I've had a particularly hard week, I start blinking the tears away.

There came a point where I realized I'd need to either embrace the craziness of our family rhythm or beg Marcus to become an insurance salesman. And I'm quite sure that would never happen. I knew that if I didn't make this mind set change and view our family life a little differently, I'd end up in a place of longing and bitterness. I've seen other police officers wives stay in that place of constant complaining about the job and the missed celebrations. It can seriously eat away at marriages and families, like a cloud of negative smoke that just hangs around the house and infuses the little time spent together. *I* am determined to live in a smoke-free home.

So, Sunday afternoons before Dad goes to work, we all sit at the table and have "Linner". It's a name the kids have termed for our big feast that takes place not quite at lunch time, not quite at dinner. One meal, at one table, in the presence of our one loving God giving thanks for this one life we've been given, even if it's a life a little off center.

Over the years I've actually learned to be thankful for our version of "normal". We set ourselves apart as Christians in a world that makes living our faith a daily battle. And we set ourselves apart as a family of law enforcement, carving out time for each other that works like a thread binding us together for the rest of the week, in a world that threatens our very unraveling.
I really wouldn't want it any other way.

Maybe it's because I'm just so used to it twelve years later or maybe it's the uniform. I still get butterflies in my stomach when I see him in a squad car. There's just a certain respect and powerful love that comes with the sacrifices we've made together for the job. It has affected us all, but I can see how it's made us stronger as a family.

As believers, sacrifice is something we're taught to view as a purposeful gift and as a way to truly live.

Sacrifice isn't exactly something that we do joyfully, there are still disappointments and times where his absence is palpable and we just endure. But being together again is our reward, making it count when we can. Tying that thread around each of our fingers, so we always remember even when we're apart.

Lauren Yanez, wife of Marcus Yanez, Colorado Springs Police Department

* * * * * * * * * * * * * * * * *

CHAPTER
Nine

Chapter 9

"Worry is the interest paid by those who borrow trouble."
— **George Washington**

Jamie paced the floor as she waited. Time seemed to stand still and all she could think about was the heated argument that she and Tom had gotten into earlier that evening. The door had slammed and the squall of his tires in the driveway resonated through her mind. Now hours later, the chiming of the clock and the howl of the cold, winter wind outside left her feeling empty and alone. He hadn't even left with a coat or shoes on, what would happen if he was in an accident somewhere?

Jamie sat down on the couch and opened her old, faded Bible that her grandma had given her as a child. As she thumbed through the tattered pages, it was as if God illuminated the following passage for her, *"So do not fear, for I am with you; do not be dismayed, for I am your God. I will strengthen you and help you; I will uphold you with my righteous right hand...For I am the LORD, your God, who takes hold of your right hand and says to you, Do not fear; I will help you.*" Isaiah 41:10, 13.

About that time, she heard the familiar hum of Tom's truck pulling back into the driveway. Jamie knew that God had heard and understood her anxious thoughts and that this was her opportunity to make things right between the two of them.

Lord, during those moments when worry consumes me, help me to focus on you my Rock and Sustainer. Help me to know that your love drives away all fear and that I can trust in you to bring peace in the midst of chaos. Thank you for all the times that you watch over me and give me your reassuring touch. Amen.

Worry

Finding Comfort in the midst of Chaos

I tend to be a "worry wart" so to marry someone who chose law enforcement as their career seems strange to think about now. My husband has been a Missouri State Highway Patrolman for 12 years. He has said to me on occasion that he carefully chooses what work experiences he shares with me knowing my tendencies to worry. So, when he does share an experience, I know there is a reason why he opens up.

The most recent frightening experience Bill encountered was when he had been informed of a car driving the wrong way on the interstate. He was given the approximate location and headed down that same strip of interstate to intervene. However, the car was not at the mile marker that was conveyed to him, but closer. As he headed around a curve at a high rate of speed, he was almost hit head on by *that* car. After the near miss, Bill sat in his patrol car shaking for quite some time. The wrong way driver ended up being an older gentleman suffering from Alzheimer's.

My relationship with God has certainly affected how I deal with my husband's job. I have turned to several verses in the Bible when worry has crept in. Philippians 4:6-7 says, *"Don't worry about anything, but pray about everything. With thankful hearts offer up your prayers and requests to God. Then, because you belong to Christ Jesus, God will bless you with peace that no one can completely understand. And this peace will control the way you think and feel."* 1 Peter 5:7 says *"God cares for you, so turn all your worries over to him."*

As I began to write this excerpt, I looked up several other verses that seemed helpful in regards to worry. John 14:27 says *"I give you peace, the kind of peace that only I can give. It isn't like the peace that this world can give. So don't be worried or afraid."* Finally, Proverbs 3:24 says *"you will rest without a worry and sleep soundly."*

I feel my husband and I have found a healthy balance of providing each other support as we face the daily challenges of life, including those connected to his job. And yet, I can also find comfort in God if I take the time to invite Him in when worry tries to consume my thoughts.

Jenny Lowe, spouse of Corporal Bill Lowe, Missouri State Highway Patrol

＊ ＊ ＊ ＊ ＊ ＊ ＊ ＊ ＊ ＊ ＊ ＊ ＊ ＊ ＊ ＊ ＊ ＊

We Put Our Trust in God

Our girls and I were on our way to church when my cell phone rang. It was my husband, Lynn. He was breathing hard and I could hear commotion in the background. He said, "It's alright...I'm ok." "What are you talking about?" I asked. Thinking I'd had the police radio on, I told him that we were almost at church, and that I had left the radio at home.

Lynn explained that he'd been in a shooting, but that he and the other deputies were okay. The suspect didn't make it. Myself being in law enforcement as well and not quite believing what had just happened, I asked if they needed any help with evidence or patrolling. He said they had it covered.

Dispatch had received numerous calls about a male subject shooting up the neighborhood. Lynn and the other deputies arrived. As Lynn was calling for the T.A.C. team, the suspect walked out his front door and aimed a weapon at Lynn who was taking cover on the other side of the suspect's pickup 10 yards away. All deputies opened fire. This occurred just one day before our 7th wedding anniversary.

The next day, we went to eat lunch. I was terribly quiet and stayed that way for several days. I kept looking around the house wondering what it'd have been like without Lynn – the girls without their father. I wondered how, Lynn's estranged biological son, if he found out, would've reacted knowing his real father had died, and he never made an effort to spend any time with him.

I wondered who I would've called first. I wondered if I'd have been able to sleep at night without him by my side. I wondered how many times our 4 year old daughter would've asked me "When's daddy coming home?" How our oldest daughter, 12, would've handled him not being here to horseplay with. I wondered a lot.

A few months later, Lynn took me to the scene. It was an old wood-frame house, light green with white trim. I saw where some of the bullets had penetrated the exterior. The porch had been wiped clean and there was a "For Sale" sign in the yard. I remember standing there in a daze thinking what any wife would be thinking at that moment, "Thank God..."

The following month, we attended the local police memorial service. Lynn was featured on the front page of the local newspaper carrying a red chrysanthemum in honor of our fallen officers.

People have asked us, "Don't you worry..?" We *can't*. We put our trust in God...we have to, otherwise we'd go crazy.

Serena Booth, a reserve peace officer for Caddo Mills P.D. specializing in investigation. She currently holds her Master Peace Officer and Special Investigator licenses and is the wife of Lynn Booth, Sergeant for Caddo Mills P.D., Texas

* * * * * * * * * * * * * * * * * *

CHAPTER
Ten

Chapter 10

"He who angers you, conquers you." – **Author Unknown**

I was just livid! It seemed like every time my husband and I turned on the news, someone was accusing an officer of police brutality. Worse yet, were times when an extremely radical politician or notable celebrity would pull the racial profiling card, backing their weight against the "good-ole boy" who had a gear to grind.

I couldn't stand it. In my anger I wanted to lash out at the unjust and ignorant attitudes of those who were hurling the unfair accusations.

Couldn't they see that cops and their families have feelings as well? Didn't they realize the sacrifices made in order that these naysayers could have their day in the press or in court? Had they been so blind as to completely ignore the fact that these brave men and women often deprive themselves of sleep, lose precious moments with their families, and work endless hours in order to bring closure to others who have been victimized?

Had they ever stopped to consider that officers are often shot at, spit upon, cursed out, knocked down and belittled? The thanks they receive is nothing more than a paycheck less than a glorified secretary in some posh office, and blisters on feet which have walked through miles of hot asphalt, carnage and unheard-of filth.

As I steamed over my feelings of anger and hatred, a still, small voice whispered through my thoughts, "Now you know how my Son felt."

Ugh! I felt as if I had swallowed a ton of bricks. Choking back the tears I realized that *my* sins had helped drive the nails into my precious Lord's hands. It was *my* sin that had caused Him such pain and agony.

The feelings of frustration began to melt away as I recounted the story of Jesus and the persecution that He went through in order to provide a way for me to be reconciled to my Heavenly Father.

Jesus had come willingly to earth to die for the sin of the world. He never sought a pat on the back or an "atta boy" from those he helped, but lovingly and sacrificially gave His all so that we might live.

"For God so loved the world that he gave his one and only Son, that whoever believes in him shall not perish but have eternal life. For God did not send his Son into the world to condemn the world, but to save the world through him." John 3:16-17

Anger

I Don't Really Want to Hurt My Child

Darcy's training pants were wet again. Again! As I struggled to pull down the soaking pants, I felt a rush of frustration.

"Darcy, you're supposed to come in the bathroom and go in the potty chair." As I spanked her with my hand, my tension and tiredness found an outlet. Spanking changed to hitting.

Darcy's uncontrollable screaming brought me back to reason. Seeing the red blister on her bottom, I dropped to my knees.

"I love Jesus," I sobbed. "I don't really want to hurt my child. Oh God, please help me."

As the weeks turned into months, my anger habit worsened. At times I grew so violent that I hit my toddler in the head. Other times I kicked her or slapped her face.

As a Christian for ten years, I was ashamed. *Oh, God, I prayed over and over again, please take away my anger.* Yet no matter how much I prayed, I could not control my anger and I wondered whether I might kill Darcy in one of my rages. In time, I had to be honest with myself--I was abusing her. "Oh, God, I'm a child abuser! Help me!"

I was afraid to tell Larry, my husband. *After all, he's a policeman. He's arresting people for the very things I'm doing.* I certainly couldn't tell my friends. What would they think of me? I led a Bible study. I was looked up to as a strong Christian woman. But inside I was screaming for help.

One day I realized Larry had left his off duty service revolver in the bureau drawer. Convinced God no longer loved me and had given up on me, I concluded suicide was the only answer. Then I wouldn't hurt Darcy any more. But then the thought sprang into my mind. "But if people hear a Christian like me committed suicide, what will they think of Jesus?" I couldn't bear the thought that Jesus' name would be maligned, even if I wasn't acting much like a Christian.

One day, I shared briefly with a neighbor friend about my anger. She didn't condemn me like another friend had when I'd tried to share my pain. She even indicated she sometimes felt angry towards her children too. *Oh, Lord, maybe there is hope for me after all*, I cried out when I left her house that day.

From that turning point, God began to reveal the underlying causes and the solutions for my anger little by little. And there were many. I had to learn how to identify my anger before it became destructive. I forced myself to believe God wanted to forgive me—over and over again. Reading books about disciplining children effectively, I became more consistent in responding calmly to Darcy's disobedience. She became better behaved.

I also copied verses like Ephesians 4:31 and Proverbs 10:12 onto cards, placing them in various locations throughout the house. As I took Darcy into the bathroom, I would be reminded that "Hatred stirreth up strifes; but love covereth all sins" (Proverbs 10:12 KJV). These verses helped to break my cycle of anger.

Eventually, I had the courage to share my problem with my Bible study group. James 5:16a admonishes us to "confess your faults one to another, and pray one for another, that ye may be healed..." (KJV). They prayed for me and their prayers indeed had "wonderful results."

Through a difficult process of growth of over a year, God's Holy Spirit empowered me to be the loving, patient mother that I wanted to be. I learned many principles during that time that I now share in the parenting books I've written. I also teach parenting seminars speak for women's retreats.

I'm thankful to the Lord for healing the relationship between Darcy and me. A beautiful 34-year-old, Darcy has forgiven me for the way I treated her. We share a close relationship.

Although I wondered during that unhappy time of my life whether God could ever forgive me for the horrible things I'd done, I know now that He has.

Kathy Collard Miller (www.KathyCollardMiller.com) is a popular retreat speaker and the author of 49 books including Women of the Bible: Smart Guide to the Bible (Thomas Nelson). She is the wife of D. Larry Miller, retired lieutenant Huntington Beach Police Department, Huntington Beach, CA.

* * * * * * * * * * * * * * * * * * * *

CHAPTER
Eleven

Chapter 11

"To one who has faith, no explanation is necessary. To one without faith, no explanation is possible." – **Thomas Aquinas**

We had grown up in our home town of Jackson, Missouri, never really imagining that God would move us away. Life had settled in and the everyday tasks of raising three kids and running a household left no room for surprises.

I had been employed for a little over four years as an Administrative Assistant to the Prosecuting Attorney for our county, when out of the blue I received a call about a job opportunity two hours north. It would be a lot more pay with benefits that were simply irresistible.

After the shock wore off and reality set it, Rick and I drove to St. Louis for me to do the interview and for him to scout around the area for local police departments. Days later, I would find out that the job opening had been given to someone within the company. I was disappointed, but figured that it was God's way of saying, "Not right now."

Several weeks went by without a passing thought, until the phone rang. It was Chief Don Fowler from the Union Police Department asking Rick if he would like to come for an interview. What?! Thinking the matter had already been settled, we had completely set aside the notion of moving away. Our family, my parents in particular, had not been thrilled with the possibility of losing their grandbabies to a far away land. How would we even begin to tell them that once again it might be a reality?

Rick made plans for the interview and headed up the interstate. Several miles and many thoughts into his travels, he pulled over and told God, "If this is your will, then send me a sign." He pulled back onto the highway and at that moment a rainbow as big as life, peered over the horizon. It was looking more and more like we would be moving north.

After many more phone calls, interviews, tests and visits, we moved Rick to Union, Missouri, to live until the house could be sold and our family could join him. For four months, he travelled back and forth between homes. It wasn't easy, but through those times we saw the Lord's hand upon it.

Not long after, God found us a buyer for our home and we were on our way to starting a new life in different surroundings. All it took was one big u-haul and a whole lot of faith, but God's been blessing us ever since.

Doubt sees the obstacles. Faith sees the way. Doubt sees the darkest night. Faith sees the day. Doubt dreads to take a step. Faith soars on high. Doubt questions "Who believes"? Faith answers "I". - Author Unknown

Faith

Responding to God's Call

Trust in the LORD with all your heart and lean not on your own understanding; in all your ways acknowledge him, and he will make your paths straight. Proverbs 3:5-6

Randy was employed with the Baltimore County Maryland Police Dept for 20 years. He had a wonderful career. For the first 10 years he led a local chapter of the Fellowship of Christian Peace Officers, which held monthly prayer breakfasts and a yearly retreat to Word of Life camp at Schroon Lake, New York.

I supported Randy at all of these functions, even after we started having children. We felt that the weekend retreat was important to our marriage and a good witness to others. Our parents were willing to baby-sit, and yes, it was a little scary leaving an infant for a trip 8 hours away, but the Lord always blessed it.

I have always been faithful in the area of hospitality when Randy has invited officers over for dinner in an effort to be a witness to them, though not my spiritual gift! At one time we lived in a very small house and Randy had a weekly Bible study and accountability session with another police officer. I agreed to leave the home for that one hour each week.

As we approached the end of our career and ministry with the Baltimore County Police Department, we began praying for what our next assignment would be. As time went by it became clear that the Lord was calling us to campus policing in the Commonwealth of Virginia. As the plans were being made, many friends and relatives questioned the wisdom of moving to another state where we knew no-one, and with the added responsibility of having two teenagers at home.

The two of us fervently prayed and stepped out in faith. Though the job was slow in coming, it did come through. Our family made the move and the Lord blessed. Both teenagers blossomed in many ways. Our oldest, who could not find a job in Maryland now has two jobs in Virginia and is attending Community College. Because of my love for dancing, I landed a position teaching a dance style aerobics at a local health club. This has opened many opportunities to minister to the women in my class.

Sometimes we must make hard decisions that others will not understand. But as long as we are faithful to God's call on our lives, then we will find contentment. That does not mean that there will not be trials along the way, but God is faithful to see us through.

Kim Brashears and her husband Lt. Randy Brashears, Commander of Investigations, University of Virginia Police Dept.

About the Author

Kristi Neace is a highly recommended speaker and author. Using her high energy, high impact, yet down-to-earth style, she motivates and encourages women of all ages to live a life in step with God's Word.

With over ten years of ministry experience, she speaks to hundreds of women throughout the year, and currently serves as member of the Women's Ministry Team for the State of Missouri, Baptist Convention.

Kristi is author of Between Friends: A Woman's Look at Mentoring God's Way, and numerous other articles.
She and her family call Missouri home.

www.kristineace.com

8239448R0

Made in the USA
Charleston, SC
21 May 2011